YPS

ADAPTED TO SURVIVE

ANIMALS THAT RUN

Angela Royston

Raintree

Raintree is an imprint of Capstone Global Library Limited, a company incorporated in England and Wales having its registered office at 7 Pilgrim Street, London, EC4V 6LB – Registered company number: 6695582

www.raintreepublishers.co.uk
myorders@raintreepublishers.co.uk

Text © Capstone Global Library Limited 2014
First published in hardback in 2014
The moral rights of the proprietor have been asserted.

Edited by Dan Nunn, Rebecca Rissman, and Helen Cox Cannons
Designed by Joanna Hinton-Malivoire
Picture research by Mica Brancic
Originated by Capstone Global Library Ltd
Production by Helen McCreath
Printed and bound in China

ISBN 978 1 406 27087 7
17 16 15 14 13
10 9 8 7 6 5 4 3 2 1

British Library Cataloguing in Publication Data
A full catalogue record for this book is available from the British Library.

Acknowledgements
We would like to thank the following for permission to reproduce photographs: Corbis pp. 25, 29 bottom right (© George H.H. Huey); Getty Images p. 27 (Universal Images Group/Auscape); Naturepl.com pp. 6 (© Jabruson), 7 (© Bryan and Cherry Alexander), 8, 20 (© Tony Heald), 13 (© B&S Draker), 14 (© Eric Baccega), 16 (© Carol Walker), 22 (© Visuals Unlimited), 24 (© Bernard Castelein), 26 (© Ingo Arndt); Shutterstock pp. 5, 29 top right (© Villiers Steyn), 15 (© Dennis Donohue), 19 (© Howard Sandler), 23 (© Linda Bucklin), 29 bottom left (© Eric Isselee); SuperStock pp. 4 (Belinda Images), 9 (Gallo Images), 10 (Corbis), 11, 12 (Minden Pictures), 17 (imagebroker.net/Alessandra Sarti/imag), 18 (age fotostock/Berndt Fischer), 21, 29 top left (age fotostock).

Cover photograph of a horse running reproduced with permission of Getty Images (Iconica/Arctic-Images).

We would like to thank Michael Bright for his invaluable help in the preparation of this book.

Every effort has been made to contact copyright holders of material reproduced in this book. Any omissions will be rectified in subsequent printings if notice is given to the publisher.

Disclaimer

Some words are shown in bold, **like this**. You can find out what they mean by looking in the glossary.

CONTENTS

GOOD AT RUNNING

Some large animals, such as horses and camels, can run very fast. Some small animals can also run fast for their size. Why and how do they run so well?

RUNNING TO SURVIVE

Animals run fast because it helps them to **survive**. Many animals **stalk** and chase other animals to eat. They need to run fast to catch their **prey**! Most of the animals they chase can also run fast, but not all.

gnu

wild dogs

Hunters pick on young and injured animals that cannot run so well, like this newborn baby reindeer.

ADAPTED TO RUN

Adaptations are special things about an animal's body that help it to **survive**. Fast runners often have a slender, **streamlined** body and long legs. Running takes a lot of energy.

impala

Champion runners

Cheetahs can reach speeds of 113 kilometres (70 miles) per hour. That is as fast as a car on the motorway!

CHEETAHS

The cheetah is the fastest land animal on Earth. It runs fast to catch its **prey**. Its spine stretches and bends so that its strong back legs cover the ground in huge strides. Its long tail helps it to balance.

long tail

Faster than a sports car

A cheetah can reach its top speed in just 3 seconds. After sprinting less than a minute, however, it runs out of breath and collapses!

GAZELLES AND PRONGHORNS

Gazelles are small antelopes. They can run fast and change direction quickly. This helps them to escape from cheetahs and other **predators**. Pronghorns can sprint at up to 100 kilometres (62 miles) per hour, but they can keep running for several kilometres at 65 kilometres (40 miles) per hour.

gazelle

pronghorn

WOLVES

Wolves often run long distances, hunting for food. Wolves have long legs and big front feet. They spread their toes and use their claws to grip the ground. Wolves often hunt together to run down **prey**.

A group of wolves is called a pack.

Long distance champion
Wolves can run up to 96 kilometres (60 miles) in one night. This is farther than two marathon races!

GALLOPING HORSES

In the past, wild horses ran fast to escape from wolves and other **predators**. They have long, thin legs, and strong **muscles** in their shoulders and hips. Today, the fastest horses are racehorses.

Racehorses are trained to run fast and can gallop at up to 70 kilometres (43 miles) per hour.

HARES

long back legs

Hares are well **adapted** for moving fast. Their power comes from their longer back legs and back feet. They quickly hop to escape from danger. A snowshoe hare has extra-long back feet. These act like **snowshoes** to stop the hare sinking into the snow.

Snowshoe hares live in parts of North America that are snowy all winter.

OSTRICHES

Most birds escape from **predators** by flying away, but ostriches are too big and heavy to fly. Instead, they use their long, thin legs to run away from lions and other predators.

Ostriches use their wings to help them slow down.

DID YOU KNOW?
An ostrich can run at up to 70 kilometres (43 miles) per hour – faster than any other two-legged animal, including humans!

FASTEST LIZARD

Lizards run to escape from **predators**. A collared lizard is a very fast lizard. Instead of running on all four legs, it stands up and runs on its two back legs. It uses its long tail to help it balance when it runs.

A collared lizard takes huge strides on its back legs. Its long claws grip the ground.

Fast dinosaur?

A collared lizard looks like a dinosaur called Compsognathus. Many scientists think that Compsognathus was the fastest of all the dinosaurs.

CRABS

A crab moves fast to escape from danger. It has eight legs, four on each side of its body. It usually runs sideways, because that is how its legs bend. Ghost crabs are one of the fastest moving crabs. When they move fast, they lift their four back legs off the ground and run on their four front legs.

Fastest crab
A ghost crab can run at nearly 4 metres (13 feet) per second. That's fast!

INSECTS

Most insects fly away from danger, but wingless insects cannot. Some run fast instead. An Australian tiger beetle runs 171 times its own length in a second. If people could do the same, we would sprint at an amazing 1,200 kilometres (746 miles) per hour!

A tiger beetle moves fast by running on just two of its six legs.

Australian tiger beetle

ANIMAL CHALLENGE

1. Most crabs do not run fast. What do they have instead that protects them from **predators** such as fish?

2. Which do you think can run faster – an elephant or a giraffe? Why?

3. Many animals that live on flat grassy plains can run fast. Why do you think that is?

Invent your own animal runner. You can use the **adaptations** shown in the photos, or you can make up some of your own.

long, thin legs

muscly shoulders

long tail

lots of legs

Answers to Animal Challenge

1. Crabs have a hard shell and two sharp claws to protect themselves from predators.
2. Giraffes have long, slim legs and can run faster than elephants. Elephants are heavy, with stout legs.
3. There are few trees and bushes on grassy plains, so there are few places to hide. Animals have to run away from danger.

GLOSSARY

adaptation special thing about an animal's body that helps it to survive in a particular way or in a particular habitat

adapted well suited to a particular activity or way of living

muscle fleshy part of the body that makes a particular part of the body move

predator animal that hunts and kills other animals for food

prey animal that is hunted and eaten by another animal

snowshoes large flat shoes that help a person to walk over snow without sinking into it

stalk to follow an animal or person, often without being seen

streamlined smooth, pointed shape that moves through air or water easily

survive manage to go on living

FIND OUT MORE

BOOKS

Cheetahs (Animal Lives), Sally Morgan (QED, 2008)

Ostrich (A Day in the Life: Grassland Animals), Louise Spilsbury (Raintree, 2012)

Wild Horses (Animal Lives), Sally Morgan (QED, 2008)

WEBSITES

kids.nationalgeographic.com/kids/animals/creaturefeature
This website gives information and photos for particular animals, including cheetahs, giraffes, and jackrabbits (hares).

www.bbc.co.uk/nature/adaptations/Running
This BBC website includes several short videos about how cheetahs, collared lizards, and other animals are adapted to run.

www.ypte.org.uk/animal-facts.php
Find out more about many different animals on this website.

INDEX